Bishop Hare's Indian Boarding Schools in South Dakota

BISHOP HARE'S INDIAN BOARDING SCHOOLS IN SOUTH DAKOTA

By FREDERICK FOOTE JOHNSON

THE RIGHT REVEREND WILLIAM HOBART HARE, D. D.
BISHOP 1873—1909

Note

THE purpose of this letter is to keep our benefactors informed of the progress of our schools and to insure that our friends shall know that we are sensible of their interest, and desire not to be forgotten.

It is not an unnatural wish of many of those who support scholarships that particular children shall be named and assigned to them as their special protegés ; but to comply is hardly practicable. The children are apt to be already named when admitted to the schools ; we need, in many cases, the liberty to keep a child for a few months only, and then supply his place by another ; and while we are sure that the boarding-schools will, as a whole, be a rich blessing, and can therefore guarantee that money given in their behalf will be productive, we cannot insure that any particular child, a small fraction of the whole, will turn out in a way to give satisfaction to those who have chosen him as the object of their hopes and charity. Further, the special attentions which benefactors are apt to bestow upon their particular protegés tend often to spoil the favored children, and to produce discontent in others. We trust, therefore, that our benefactors will ask to name only the scholarship which they support, and not the child who occupies it, and look for their satisfaction, not to good results in the case of a particular child, which must be an uncertainty, but to the good effect of the schools as a whole, which is a blessed certainty.

Sioux Falls, S. D., April, 1910.

ST. MARY'S GIRLS AT PLAY

Bishop Hare's Indian Boarding Schools in South Dakota

By FREDERICK FOOTE JOHNSON

IT is now almost five years ago that I journeyed over for the first time to make a visitation as assistant to the beloved Bishop of South Dakota among our Sioux Indian brethren of the Church west of the Missouri River. Thirty miles from any railway point, in the midst of the unbroken prairie, in the evening when the Chapel service was over, in a rude, one-roomed log cabin lighted by a dingy lamp, with a fringe of Indian men about me on the cabin floor, I sat and listened for the first time to the Sioux Indian tongue.

I shall never forget the weirdness of the cabin nor the native dignity of the several speakers as each stood up to address me, nor the picturesqueness of the language as it came to me through my interpreter. Presently, after many had told out their hearts, an old Indian Chief arose to tell me something of the story of the coming of the Gospel to the people of the Dakotas. "A few years ago," said he, "we Indians just like this cabin if you put out that light. We all dark and desolate and dreary. Bishop Hare, he come to us. He build us schools for our children. He bring us Holy Baptism and Confirmation and Holy Communion. He give us Bible and Prayer Book. He build us churches and chapels. He send us teachers and ministers of Jesus. Now we Indians like this cabin with that lamp upon the wall; *we all getting light.*"

As I look out from my window in Sioux Falls to-day upon the pansy-covered mound above the grave in which the body of the Bishop of South Dakota rests—"The inn of a pilgrim on his journey to Jerusalem,"—I say to myself: When the new series of the stories of the triumphs of Christian faith is written, it will tell the story of how the young man, gently born, fine-fibred, delicately reared, splendidly educated, gat him out of his country, and from his kindred, and from his father's house, unto a land which God would show him. It will tell how, leaving the attractive intellectual atmosphere and social advantages and opportunities of a cultured eastern city, he built his cabin-home in the Dakota Territory, a waste of barren prairie, roamed over by wild nomad buffaloes and wild nomad Sioux. It will tell how, when many good people were saying, "What's the use of preaching the Gospel to a perishing race," he persisted in his mission, because he heard the cry of them that were in captivity and longed to deliver a people appointed unto death. It will tell how, when people everywhere who had no experimental knowledge

4

of the proposition were saying, "No good Indian but a dead Indian," he, with a noble band of clergy and other teachers whom he grappled to his heart with hooks of steel, in the land of the Dakotas builded out of almost hopeless material a spiritual house able to resist storms; settled the roving Sioux Indian in families, and made countless numbers of them earnest and devoted and consistent followers and teachers of the gentle Jesus.

On the white-metal cross which the Bishop used to give to each person on whom he laid his hands in Confirmation among the people of the Dakotas is inscribed the words, «Ἵνα ζωὴν ἔχωσι.» "That they might have life." He, following his Master, gave life. Six and thirty years of life he joyously gave for the spiritual and moral and physical and intellectual and material upbuilding of the Sioux—for no interest of the Sioux to him was foreign. And when, in last October, God's finger touched him and he slept, I verily believe that the final paragraph of the most splendid chapter in the history of nineteenth century missions in America was closed.

OLD WIND SOLDIER
Facing the setting sun

5

THE LITTLE BOYS OF ST. ELIZABETH'S

In 1873 Bishop Hare came out to this western land as the missionary bishop of Niobrara. He found 6,000 Indian children running wild, like jack-rabbits on the plains. It was before the Government began to make provision for the education of the Indian. Bishop Hare immediately appealed to the Church for financial help, and boarding schools were built, whose names are household words in the homes of many of the devoted and generous churchfolk of our land: St. Mary's and St. Elizabeth's.

St. Mary's is for girls only. It is situated on the great Rosebud Reserve, 35 miles from the nearest railway point, which is a point called Valentine, in Nebraska. This year the enrollment at St. Mary's is 75. The report for the month of March has just this moment come to my desk, and shows an average attendance of 70. One girl enrolled is 17; two

ST. MARY'S SCHOOL

are 16; the others are aged from 5 to 15. Some of the little people who read this booklet may be interested to hear the names of some of the girls of St. Mary's. Here they are: Nellie At-the-Straight, Julia Bear-Doctor, Nellie Brave-Boy, Millie First-in-Trouble, Carrie Gunhammer, Louise Picket-pin, Clara Points-at-Him, Nellie Pretty-Voice-Eagle, Rosa Quick-Bear, Mabel Six-Shooter. There are other names which you would think just as queer.

The Principal of St. Mary's, Mr. L. K. Travis, and his good wife, are just completing their ninth year of efficient service at that splendid lighthouse out on the billowy South Dakota prairie. There are seven assistants to the principal at St. Mary's, two of whom are also pupils of the school. The following extract from a letter of Mr. Travis may be of interest:

"The school keeps five or six horses; four cows, which furnish milk for the school and sufficient cream and butter for cooking and family use; hens enough to supply eggs during nearly all the year, and about twenty hogs. Four

7

heifers are now being raised to replace the milch cows as they are needed.

"A kitchen garden is cultivated which yields an abundance of vegetables during the season. Several hundred bushels of potatoes are grown, which abundantly supply the school the entire school-year.

"In the last two years considerable new ground has been broken, so that the general farming land for the growing of oats, corn, millet, etc., now includes about fifty acres. We cut and store for winter use fifty or sixty tons of tame hay.

"As we have no boys at St. Mary's, these outside operations depend upon the labor of the regular farmer with the assistance of the principal and a small amount of outside help required at harvest time."

I have told you that St. Mary's School is in the south part of South Dakota, about 25 miles from the Nebraska line. It is for Indian girls only. St. Elizabeth's school is away up in the northern end of the state, on the Standing Rock Reserve, about 25 miles from the North Dakota line. It is for Indian boys and girls. A monthly report which falls under my eye as I write gives an enrollment of 25 boys and 37 girls; a total of 62, with an average of 60.5. I am tempted to ask whether the averages in white schools at the East

ST. ELIZABETH'S MISSION

Sewing Class for Little Girls with Pupil Teachers at St. Mary's School

put us very much to shame? Two boys at St. Elizabeth's are 17 years of age. The youngest lad is 8. The oldest girl at St. Elizabeth's is 17, and the youngest is 6. And these boys and girls have just the same kind of names as the St. Mary's girls—I mean just as funny. The Principal of St. Elizabeth's, Mr. J. L. Ricker, has completed his third year of efficient service. In addition to his good wife he has a staff of five assistants. In a recent letter Mr. Ricker says: "Our children have all returned to school well and happy and everything is running as smoothly as it is possible to run. Everybody is working hard, for at this time of the year there is so much to be done in a school of this kind."

St. Elizabeth's has a railway station of the new Chicago, Milwaukee & Puget Sound Railway about two miles distant. In a few weeks through trains from Chicago to

Seattle will pass almost through the front yard of the school. This sometimes seems to some of us a doubtful benefit. But the youngsters don't agree with us on that point, for they like to sit on the fence and watch the train whiz by.

But I would not have you think that all the time is spent in sitting on the fence. The boys have many busy hours each day: farming, gardening, splitting and fetching wood and hauling water. The girls (both at St. Elizabeth's and at St. Mary's) learn bread-making, cooking, laundering, general housework, sewing, mending, dress-making, and fancy work. In both schools faithful and painstaking class-room work is done under the patient and gentle guidance of the kindly teachers. Reading, writing, arithmetic and geography are taught. There are hymn-singing, and Bible lessons, and Catechism drill. There is bright and happy worship morning and evening in the school chapels. And on Sundays the children and their teachers meet with the congregations which assemble regularly in the nearby church. Well-dressed, bright-faced, clean-bodied, happy-hearted children are they all; learning lessons and forming habits which will make them useful citizens of the state; and learning also those things which a Christian ought to know and believe to his soul's health.

To help in the support of these Indian Boarding Schools, Bishop Hare instituted the system of Scholarships which has been in use for many years. He estimated that the annual payment of $60 would cover the expenses of a pupil in the schools. Parishes, Sunday-schools, branches of the Auxiliary and of the Juniors, and individuals here and there, have generously taken many Scholarships and carried them on from year to year.

In the example of the noble Bishop Hare, who in this western field laid down his life for his friends, we have a compelling illustration of what one man considered the cause of Christian missions was worthy of in the way of personal service, personal sacrifice; in the way of life, and love, and labor.

Are there not many who read these lines who will make glad thank-offerings to God for this choice vessel of His grace, and who, from their " much " or from their " little," will send their gifts to carry on the work from which he rests?

The Greatest of Treats— Bishop Hare's Visit

❡ Letters and freight for St. Mary's School should be addressed Rosebud Agency, South Dakota, via Valentine, Nebraska.

❡ Letters and freight for St. Elizabeth's School should be directed to Wakpala, Boreman County, South Dakota.

SCHOLARSHIPS

St. Mary's School (for Girls), Rosebud Agency, S. Dakota

SHARES, EACH, SIXTY DOLLARS PER ANNUM

NAME OF SHARE	SUPPORTED BY
1 R C Rogers	"A Member," Holy Apostles', New York, through Niobrara League.
2 J P. Lundy	"A Member," Holy Apostles', New York, through Niobrara League
3 Sarah Whitman Bible Class	Trinity Church, through Dakota League, Boston, Mass
4 Calvary	Calvary Sunday-school, Germantown, Philadelphia, Pa
5 St. Luke's........	St Luke's Sunday-school, Montclair, N. J.
6 Sophie	(Endowed) The late Mrs John Carter Brown, Providence, R I
7 Christ Church	Christ Church Sunday-school, New York, N. Y
8 H. H Houston	St Peter's Sunday-school, Germantown, Philadelphia, Pa
9 St John's Sunday School .	St. John's Sunday-school, Providence, R I
10 G J. Greer (In Memoriam)	Zion and St Timothy's, New York, through Niobrara League
11 Lucretia M Dexter (In Memoriam)	Henry Dexter, New York, N. Y.
12 Mary E Hinman (In Memoriam)	(Endowed.) Members of the Indian League Assn
13 Grace H Hamlen Memorial . ..	Members Dakota League, and personal Friends, Massachusetts
14 Bishop McLaren	Through Chicago Branch Junior Auxiliary.
15 Cotheal Memorial ...	Miss E. Cotheal, New York, through Niobrara League
16 St George's . .	St George's, New York, through Niobrara League
17 Compo	Mrs. William R McCready and Mrs John B Morris, St Bartholomew's, New York, thro' Niobrara League.
18 Charles Easton	Mrs Edward Fuller, Church of the Incarnation, New York (Endowed)
19 Dr A T Twing	"A Friend,' New York, N Y.(Endowed)
20 Henry Herbert Smythe	"A Member," Trinity Church, Boston, Mass , through Woman's Auxiliary
21 Mortimer Memorial	(Endowed) The late Miss Matilda S Mortimer, New York, N Y
22 James R Swords (In Memoriam)	Miss P C Swords, Trinity Chapel, N Y , thro Nio. Lg
23 Frances Lathrop Fiske	Rev. George S Fiske, St John's (East) Boston, Mass , through Women's Auxiliary
24 Rev Dr E A Bradley	St Agnes' Chapel, New York, Woman's Auxiliary, through Niobrara League
25 Holy Trinity	Holy Trinity, Indians' Hope Association, Phila , Pa
26 Grace M. Lane ...	Mrs Edward V. Z Lane, Church of the Incarnation, New York, through Niobrara League
27 Laura Davis (In Memoriam)	Philadelphia, Pa (Endowed)
28 Sarah Swayne	Mrs Edward Parsons, New York, N Y
29 Harry and Louise (In Memoriam)	"Faith," St James' Church, Zanesville, Ohio
30 Cora Lyman (In Memoriam) . .	"A Member," Trinity Church, Boston, Mass , Woman's Auxiliary
31 Calvary	Calvary Sunday-school, Pittsburg, Pa
32 Swannanoa	"A Member," Trinity Church, Boston, Mass , through Woman's Auxiliary.

33 David J Elv Memorial   . ..   (Endowed) The late Mrs D J Elv, Church of the
    Incarnation, New York, N Y

34 William M Dane .... Memorial, Junior Auxiliary, Baltimore, Md

35 St Agnes .... St Agnes' Chapel, "A Member," through Niobrara
    League, New York, N.Y

36 Jeannie Alston)
37 Little Anna   ) . • ....Grace Church, Richmond, Va

38 The Drifton . . . St James', Infant School of Mrs. Eckley B Coxe, Drif-
    ton, Pa

39 Shrewsbury . . Shrewsbury Br Woman's Auxiliary, Shrewsbury, Md

4C —————— . ... Smith College, Missionary Society Northampton, Mass

41 Indians' Hope . Indians' Hope Association, Diocese of Pennsylvania

42 Mary H Rochester . .... Southern Ohio Branch Woman's Auxiliary

43 Bishop McCormick . . ... Western Michigan Branch Woman's Auxiliary

44 Annie Flower Paul . Christ Church Sunday-school, Philadelphia, Pa

45 Loving Mother . Miss S E Whittemore, Chairman Dakota League, Mass

46 Mary M Jines ... . Newark Branch Woman's Auxiliary

St. Elizabeth's School (for Boys and Girls), Standing Rock Reserve, S. Dakota

SHARES, EACH, SIXTY DOLLARS PER ANNUM

NAME OF SHARE	SUPPORTED BY
1 Richard Newton ..	"A Friend," Texas
2 Meredith Norris (In Memoriam)	Endowed by Mrs John Markoe, Philadelphia, Pa
3 Walter Nichols Hart . .	(Endowed) A Lady, through Woman's Auxiliary.
4 "M. M. E" (In Memoriam).	The Rev Alfred L Elwin, Philadelphia, Pa
5 Charlotte Augusta Astor (In Mem)	The Lenten Indian League of N Y, thro' Niob League
6 All Saints'	All Saints' Sunday-school, Frederick Md
7 Ivy Lyons (In Memoriam) .	(Endowed)—[Half Scholarship]
8 Bishop Bass	Ladies of St Paul's, Newburyport, Mass
9 Bishop Randall ...	Messiah Sunday school, Boston, Mass
10 Arthur Brooks	Church of the Incarnation, New York, thro' Niob League
11 Joseph B Collins	"A Friend," New York (Endowed)
12 Nellie Rogers Robinson	St Andrew's, Louisville Ky., through Woman's Aux
13 Trinity Memorial	"A Member," Trinity Church Moorestown, N J
14 George L Williams	Mrs L Williams, Transfiguration, New York, through Niobrara League
15 Ellen F Robinson . ..	Western Michigan Branch Woman's Auxiliary
16 Harvey M Nelson .	}Miss Nelson, Grace Church, New York, through Niobrara League
17 Emily Nelson (In Memoriam)	
18 William Reed Huntington .	
19 Rev Dr John W Brown .	Ladies' Missionary Society, St Thomas', New York, through Niobrara League
20 St Mark's ..	St Mark's, Philadelphia, Pa
21 Charlotte	"M C S," New York
22 St Luke's .	St Luke's & Epiphany, through Indians' Hope Association, Philadelphia, Pa
23 Tuxedo .	St Mary' Sunday-school, Tuxedo, N Y, thro' Nio Lg.
24 James M Cushman ..	Miss Cushman, Holy Apostles, New York, thro' Nio Lg.
25 Newark . . .	Newark Branch Junior Auxiliary

lice Rives	Miss Ellen King, Washington, D C
avid H Greer	St Bartholomew's Parish House, Miss Squires' Primary Class, New York.
lizabeth M Graff	Indians' Hope Association, under the will of Mrs. Graff, Philadelphia, Pa.
ishop Hare	Holy Trinity, "Two Members," through Indians' Hope Association, Philadelphia, Pa.
illiam B Bourne	Church of the Saviour, Philadelphia, (West) Pa., through Indians' Hope Association
dwin Parsons	Mrs Edwin Parsons, New York, N Y.
ll Saints' Day...	St Paul's, Stockbridge, Mass
e Witt (In Memoriam) ...	Holy Innocents' Sunday-school, Albany, N Y.
dward C Clark (In Memoriam)	(Endowed) " Mrs E. M C ," Waterbury, Ct.
ishop Lines	Woman's Missionary League, Diocese of Newark.
eorge H Houghton	(Endowed) The late Mrs J J. Astor, New York, N Y
r Cuming	Woman's Auxiliary, Diocese of Western Michigan.
ev Geo. Murdock (In Memoriam)	"L," Woman's Auxiliary, Diocese of Washington
hio	Ohio Branch Woman's Auxiliary.
t. John's ....St	John's Sunday-school, Stamford, Conn.
esse S Bonsall	(Endowed) The late Mrs. S. R. Bonsall, Frederick, Md
eorge L. Harrison Number 2 .	A member of the Church, Philadelphia, Pa.
livia M. Cutting	Christ Church, New York, through Niobrara League
eorge C. Morris	(Endowed) "A Member," St Peter's, Philadelphia, Pa.
race Chantry	Grace Chantry Sunday-school, New York
hristian Mason Gibson Memorial	(Endowed) The late Mrs. W F. Cochran, New York, through Niobrara League
enry Lubeck . . .	David Clarkson, Zion and St. Timothy's, New York, through Niobrara League.
unior Aux of St Peter's Church Germantown .	⎰ The Young Woman's Chapter and the Little Sisters of the Church, Chapters of the Junior Auxiliary, St Peter's Church, Germantown, Philadelphia, Pa , through Indians' Hope Association
irginia . . . .(Endowed	) Mrs St. Geo T Campbell, Philadelphia, Pa
ishop Dudley . ..	Christ Church Sunday-school, Nashville, Tenn
B G . . .	St. James', Indians' Hope Association, Philadelphia, Pa
ary H W Silvester Memorial	Advocate Memorial, Philadelphia, Pa , through Indians' Hope Association
———— . ..	Grace, W A , New Orleans, La
hurch of the Ascension	Church of the Ascension, N Y , thro' Niobrara League

Graduate Scholarships

ED FOR THE SUPPORT OF INDIAN YOUNG MEN WHO, HAVING BEEN
AT LEAST PARTIALLY EDUCATED, ARE NOW WORKING AS
HELPERS, CATECHISTS AND DEACONS

enry M Beare .	Miss Helen King, Washington, D C
lfred M Randolph	Ladies of Emmanuel Church, Baltimore, Md
homas Streatfield Clarkson (In Memoriam)	⎱ Miss Lavinia Clarkson, Potsdam, N Y
evinus Clarkson (In Memoriam) ⎰	

14

5 Lenten League . ...The Lenten Indian League, of New York, through Niobrara League
6 St. Michael's . ...St Michael s Sunday-school, Bristol, R I
7 George Zabriskie Gray ... ..St. John's Memorial, Cambridge, Mass
8 Cornelius Kingsland Memorial ... Mrs W. M. Kingsland, Grace Church, New York, through Niobrara League
9 Bishop Burgess .. .. .. St Asaph's Sunday-school, Bala, Pa
10 James M Lawton (In Memoriam) Grace Church, New York, Mrs J M Lawton, through Niobrara League
11 Covenant . Covenant, through Indians' Hope Association, Philadelphia, Pa
12 Phillips Brooks . ... " A Friend, ' St Paul s, Stockbridge, Mass
13 Theodore Crane Andrews(In Mem) Mrs William L. Andrews, Church of the Incarnation, New York, through Niobrara League
14 Robert Anderson (In Memoriam) Grace Church, New York, Mrs James M Lawton, through Niobrara League
15 John Andrews Harris .. St Paul's, through Indians' Hope Association, Philadelphia (Chestnut Hill), Pa
16 Paulo Post (In Memoriam) ..."A Member," Holy Trinity Church, Philadelphia, Pa
17 The Misses Masters School The Misses Masters School, Dobbs Ferry, N Y
18 George L Harrison Number 1 A member of the Church, Philadelphia, Pa
19 William Woodward .. . ... St Peter's Sunday-school, Baltimore, Md
20 Alonzo Potter . . Grace Church, Indian Committee, New York.
21 Bishop Bedell... .. .. "A Friend,' New York (Endowed.)
22 M A. DeW Howe . . Bishop Stevens and Henry Spackman Bible-classes, St Luke's Church, Philadelphia, (Kensington), Pa
23 Church of the Saviour .... Church of the Saviour Sunday-school, Philadelphia, (W), Pa
24 Bertha . . . "A Member," St Luke's, Montclair, N J, through Woman's Auxiliary
25 St Elizabeth . ... St Asaph's Sunday-school, Bala, Pa
26 Mary Spingler Van Beuren (In Mrs Fred T Van Beuren, Church of the Ascension, Memoriam) . .. New York, through Niobrara League
27 Schmelzel Memorial .. Miss Jane E Schmelzel, New York, through Niobrara League
28 William Mercer Grosvenor .. Incarnation, Missionary League, New York, N Y , Niobrara League
29 Percy Browne . St James' Sunday-school, Boston (Highlands), Mass
30 C C. Tiffany .... Zion and St Timothy's, through Niobrara League, New York, N Y
31 Bishop Brewer Trinity Sunday-school, Watertown, N. Y.
32 Bishop Doane .... St. Peter's, Woman's Auxiliary, Albany, N Y.
33 Samuel Lawrence (In Memoriam) Mrs S Lawrence, Church of the Transfiguration, New York, N Y , through Niobrara League (Endowed)
34 Thomas Balch (In Memoriam) Endowed by Miss F W Balch, Philadelphia, Pa
35 Rev H. E Montgomery ... A Member of the Woman's Auxiliary, New York, N Y , through Niobrara League
36 Wm Lewis Morris, Jr , (In Mem) Mrs George Cabot Ward, Church of the Incarnation, New York, N Y , through Niobrara League
37 Morris and Cora McGraw Memorial Annunciation, Miss Cora McGraw, Woman's Auxiliary, New Orleans, La
38 Frederick F Johnson . . ..Miss Alice L Lane, through Niobrara League, New York.
39 Lindsay Parker. . . St Peter's Sunday-school, Brooklyn, N Y
40 William Hobart Hare .. ..."L," Chicago, Ill

15

[1] 6 10 C P 3 m